ON TRACK FOR GOD

ON TRACK FOR GOD

A Guide to Spirituality for Young Adults

PATRICK COGHLAN

VERITAS

Published 2008 by
Veritas Publications
7/8 Lower Abbey Street
Dublin 1
Ireland

Email publications@veritas.ie
Website www.veritas.ie

ISBN 978-1-84730-128-4

Designed by Lir Mac Cárthaigh
Printed in Ireland by ColourBooks Ltd, Dublin.

*Veritas books are printed on paper made from the wood pulp of
managed forests. For every tree felled, at least one tree is planted,
thereby renewing natural resources.*

CONTENTS

INTRODUCTION

I was eighteen at the time. It was my first trip to London on my own. Having arrived early for an appointment, I was killing time, walking around the side streets surrounded by expensive town houses and luxury motorcars. Suddenly, now that the rush and bustle of the journey was over I was feeling very alone. I might add that these were the days before mobile telephones. Then, something fluorescent caught my eye on the side of a lamppost. Stopping for a closer look, it was a sticker telling me to smile, because God loves me. No longer did I feel alone, because I knew that God was with me every step of the way.

In a world that can be very hostile and isolating at times, life can seem very lonely. But in Matthew 28:20 Jesus promises that when we follow him he is with us always: in the good and joyful times, and the difficult, sad and stressful times – strengthening, guiding, helping and loving. John 3:16 tells us that God sent Jesus into the world as a demonstration of his love for us. God still loves us all, and that is a good starting point for this journey of exploration into spirituality.

On Track for God is aimed at young adults in its approach, but it is the same Christianity that is open to everyone.

HOW-TO-USE GUIDE

< PAST – PRESENT – FUTURE >
This first section is optional, but encouraged. For this you will need a small notebook to jot notes in. It is a personal response to the triune God (God the Father, Jesus the Son and the Holy Spirit) and his word (the Bible). It involves looking back, examining the present and thinking about hopes and dreams for the future. In the first chapter we ask the question: what is your life like now? In successive chapters the approach is: has anything changed in response to God and his word?

Ask the questions
In modern society, we are told to ask questions. One or more questions are asked as a lead in to the chapter. Perhaps some of them are similar questions to ones that you have been asking ... or perhaps have been stifling.

Introduction
A brief, sometimes humorous, but poignant introductory passage leads into the key part of the chapter, which looks at the evidence available in scripture.

What the Bible says
A number of Bible passages related to the questions that have been asked are examined. One or more key verses are printed out in full from the *New International Version Bible*, followed by bullet points and notes. The verse references are given to enable you to read around them and to look up additional

notes in a study Bible or commentary. Sometimes you are advised to read, or at least look through, a wider passage.

For example
There are so many people in the Bible whose good examples we can look to. This section highlights one particular example to focus on in relation to the topic looked at in that chapter. It may or may not be someone who has been mentioned earlier.

A guide to spirituality for today's young adults
The main points of the session are summarised using bullet points.

Appendix
In this section, a meditative prayer of personal response can be found for each of the sessions. Each prayer is written out to be used either as a guide or just as it stands – as an act of personal response. There is a final session of <PAST – PRESENT – FUTURE> in the appendix, which considers the overall response. Once again, use of the appendix is optional.

1. WHAT'S IT ALL ABOUT?

< PAST – PRESENT – FUTURE >
Before looking at this session, take your notebook and spend a few minutes jotting down some notes about yourself:

- *Some memories about your past, e.g. achievements, failures, happy times, difficult or sad times, joys and regrets …*
- *Something about yourself at the moment, e.g. the job you do, family life, assessment of what you have achieved in your life so far …*
- *Hopes for the future, e.g. your aims and priorities in life, what plans you have, how you would like to see yourself in five or ten years' time …*

Ask the questions
- Is the Bible history or parables?
- Is it relevant to life in the twenty-first century?
- What does it all mean?

Introduction
Do you own a Bible? Have you taken the time to read the Bible? What is your attitude towards the Bible? Is it an object of sentimental value, stored away in a cupboard or somewhere, rather than parting with it? Do you treat it like that faithful old cookery book or encyclopaedia that you wouldn't be without, but can't recall when you last used it? Is it used to prop open a door, or level up a table with a wonky leg? Are you contemptuous of it, regarding it as out of date and irrelevant to life today? Or do you regard it in the same way as you would an invaluable

instruction manual for something highly technical, which you use on a daily basis and wouldn't be without – and much, much more? These days, I am sure we have all become accustomed to flat packing. It would appear that for cheapness and convenience an abundance of things are available in this form, ranging from furniture to bicycles, and even the humble wheelbarrow. Thankfully, the accompanying instructions now seem to be much improved – invaluable to the process of construction. I always keep instruction books in a safe place, ready for use. I look upon the Bible as being within this category of a highly valued resource – and much, much more – that I wouldn't be without. I have heard it said the best Bible to have is a *well-worn one*.

What the Bible says

All Scripture is God-breathed and is useful for teaching, rebuking, correcting and training in righteousness, so that the man of God may be thoroughly equipped for every good work. (2 Timothy 3:16-17)

- In terms of considering the Bible, this is a very fundamental passage to look at.
- The implication is that, because all Scripture is inspired by God and thus relevant to life, it has no time limit. Indeed, it applies to all generations, including today's.
- Scripture equips the reader for all aspects of life, including the setting of goals and boundaries.

Look also at verses 14 and 15.

For the word of God is living and active. Sharper than any double edged sword, it penetrates even to dividing soul and spirit, joints and marrow; it judges the thoughts and attitudes of the heart. (Hebrews 4:12)

- The Bible need not be just a book of written words; it becomes the living word of God when we act upon his promises contained within and strive to live out its teaching, in conjunction with our relationship with Jesus the Son, God the Father and the Holy Spirit. As such, it is powerful and life changing.

The disciples came to him and asked, 'Why do you speak to the people in parables?'
He replied, 'The knowledge of the secrets of the kingdom of heaven has been given to you, but not to them.' (Matthew 13:10-11)

- Jesus uses parables in his teaching; simple, everyday stories in understandable language that people will listen to with interest and comprehend at a physical level. However, within these stories also lie deep spiritual truths, built up in layers.
- The depth of spiritual understanding that the listener receives is dependant on their receptiveness and interest to learn more about the purposes of God.
- Ultimately it is God's desire to reveal himself and his intentions to us.

Look also at verses 12 and 13.

Some people suggest that certain parts of the Old Testament are parabolic rather than historic. I prefer not to enter into such discussion – I know what I believe! However, the crux is that we pick out, understand and live by the spiritual messages that are contained within scripture.

In the beginning God created the heavens and the earth. (Genesis 1:1)

Genesis is the book of beginnings:

- God creates the world.
- Humankind is created in God's image.
- Sin or disobedience to God enters into his creation and damages it.
- We see the first prediction of the coming messiah.
- God makes his first judgement.

Have a look through Genesis and pick out these and other *beginnings*. The beginnings in Genesis are themes that are continued throughout the Bible and reach a climax in the New Testament.

My ears had heard of you but now my eyes have seen you. (Job 42:5)

- In one sense, in the book of Job, we see a man dealing with the issue of suffering in his life and coming out with a stronger faith and personal relationship with God as a result.
- In a broader sense we see an eternal perspective of creation – God's creation being damaged by humankind's disobedience to him and the devil's intervention. However, through suffering and hardship many end up seeking God's forgiveness and discovering a greater and more personal knowledge of and relationship with God through faith in Jesus.

Look quickly through the book of Job; try to get the gist and feel of it.

For example

How often do you find yourself in a situation wondering what the right decision is? Maybe feeling that what you need is an instruction manual for life to give you the answers you're looking for. The Bible is just such a book. Time and time again, we see Jesus delving into scripture for his replies to people. Take a look at Matthew 4:1-11 (especially verses 4, 6 and 10).

A guide to spirituality for today's young adults

- The Bible is the inspired and living word of God.
- Focus on the spiritual messages it contains.
- Prayerfully allow God to reveal the deeper truths of Scripture to you.
- God's word is still relevant to you today – there is no sell by date!
- The Bible is not a selection of random stories – there are themes that follow through.
- Jesus sets the example of looking to scripture for answers to life's problems and to help with difficult decisions.

2. THE FAMILY RESEMBLANCE

< Past – Present – Future >
Before looking at this session, take your notebook and spend a few minutes jotting down some notes about yourself:

- *Look back to what you wrote down before the first chapter. As a result of the contents of that chapter, has anything changed in your lifestyle, attitudes, beliefs, feelings, priorities, dynamics or ambitions? If so, what has changed and how has it changed?*

Ask the questions
- Who is God?
- What is he like?

Introduction
Like it or not, we all take after our parents in some way: looks, mannerisms, temperament, behaviour, etc. Whenever a new baby is born, people gaze into the cot and declare that certain features are just like those of one of the parents or grandparents. Characteristics like premature thinning of the hair may follow the male line; I frequently promise my son that he too will lose his hair when he teases me about my baldness. Some family likenesses are hereditary, whereas some are learned. Who do you take after? Who do you strive to be like?

The responsibility of parents to set a good example and be role models to their children is tremendous. Sadly, if we're honest, those of us who are parents probably all look back and think, 'We could have done better!'

It was always God's intention that we look to him as our heavenly parent and constantly strive to be more like him, to take on more of the family resemblance.

What the Bible says

> Then God said, 'Let us make man in our image, in our likeness, and let them rule over the fish of the sea and the birds of the air, over the livestock, over all the earth, and over all the creatures that move along the ground.' (Genesis 1:26)

- Though we were created in the likeness of God, when sin entered into the world that likeness was damaged.
- God gives humankind a degree of sovereignty, with the command to rule over all living creatures.
- Just as God is creative, he has given us creative skills to use, e.g. music, art, writing, building, gardeining, cooking, etc.
- The Triune God – God the Father, Jesus the Son and the Holy Spirit – is the perfect example of relationship and love. We too have been given the ability to love and be loved and form relationships. It is God's desire that we should relate with him.
- Despite being damaged by the presence of sin in the world, God has given us a conscience to give us a sense of right and wrong. We need to look to the Bible and the power and guidance of the Holy Spirit to hone our consciences up.

> The Word became flesh and made his dwelling among us. We have seen his glory, the glory of the One and Only, who came from the Father, full of grace and truth. (John 1:14)

- What better way for God to reveal himself to his creation than through his Son appearing in human form, the one who demonstrates perfectly his nature and characteristics.

Jesus answered: 'Don't you know me, Philip, even after I have been among you such a long time? Anyone who has seen me has seen the Father. How can you say, "Show us the Father?"' (John 14:9)

- Jesus confirms that he is the exact likeness of the Father.
- It is by getting to know Jesus better that we also get to know more about the Father. This we can do by entering into a close relationship with Jesus and by learning more about him through the Bible.

But the fruit of the Spirit is love, joy, peace, patience, kindness, goodness, faithfulness, gentleness and self-control. (Galatians 5:22-23a)

- In a sense, the fruit of the Spirit is the family likeness that God desires us to demonstrate in our lives.

Read the rest of the passage Galatians 5:16-26.

For example
Take a look at Galatians 2:20. Paul sums up what it means in his life to have taken on the family likeness of God. His motivation, example and dynamic in life are so Christ-centred that he claims no longer to be governed by things like selfish ambitions, thoughts or desires. It doesn't happen all at once. We will look further at the ministry of Paul later on.

A guide to spirituality for today's young adults
- We were created in God's image. Though the image has been marred by sin, something of it still remains. It is

God's desire that you should strive constantly to take on his family likeness.

- Look to the person and life of Jesus to see God revealed.
- Get to know Jesus better.
- Prayerfully allow the Holy Spirit to work in your life, to help you demonstrate the fruit of the Spirit day by day.

3. ARE YOU RUNNING THE RACE OR RUNNING AWAY?

< PAST – PRESENT – FUTURE >
Before looking at this session, take your notebook and spend a few minutes jotting down some notes about yourself:

- *Would you like to take on more of the 'family resemblance' talked about in the previous chapter? Write down some details of what characteristics you would like to emulate.*
- *Maybe you feel that you have* already *taken on more of that resemblance since that session. If so, in what ways do you feel you have become more like God?*

Ask the questions
- What is the purpose of life?
- Why are we here?

Introduction
Are you, or were you, a sportsman or woman? The old saying used to go, 'It's not the winning that's important, it's the taking part'. Indeed, we hear marathon runners saying, 'I'm just pleased to have reached the finishing line', but in our modern society, ruthlessness has entered into many areas of the business and sporting world. We see signs of the attitude becoming 'win or achieve targets at any cost'. The consequence of failure to realise this attitude sadly often results in dismissal. We need to have goals or ambitions to give our lives purpose and motivate us, but those goals and ambitions need to be God-centred and not self-centred. They also need to be for the benefit of others and not at the expense of others. In the New Testament,

Paul frequently talks about living the Christian life in terms of running a race and reaching goals. We have a choice to make: we can either run the race, striving to live out the Christian life of love and witness, and focus on the goals that have been set before us, endeavouring to achieve them; or we can try to run away from God, and avoid making any effort whatsoever to fulfil his purposes for us.

What the Bible says

> Do you know that in a race all the runners run, but only one gets the prize? Run in such a way as to get the prize. Everyone who competes in the games goes into strict training. They do it to get a crown that will not last; but we do it to get a crown that will last forever. Therefore I do not run like a man running aimlessly. (1 Corinthians 9:24-26a)

- Paul is not encouraging ruthlessness or cheating in order to win the prize at any cost; nor is he saying that there is no value in running the race unless we come first. Instead, he is simply advocating that the race be taken seriously, and we give it our best effort. The Christian life of love and witness should not be taken on lightly!
- Following on from that, it is necessary to prepare for any sporting competition. Just as in order to prepare for the Christian life we need faith in Jesus, a good knowledge of scripture, a solid prayer life and openness to the Holy Spirit working in and through us.
- There is often a reward for all those who complete something like a marathon race – a medal, certificate or t-shirt. Paul emphasises that though we might proudly show off such things, there is a transient nature to them, unlike the reward that Jesus' followers will receive when they complete their race, or reach their goal, of living out the Christian life of love and witness.

Therefore, since we are surrounded by such a great cloud of witnesses, let us throw off everything that hinders and the sin that so easily entangles, and let us run with perseverance the race marked out for us. (Hebrews 12:1)

- Paul emphasises the need for the same kind of perseverance as we live out the Christian life as is necessary for running a marathon – especially as the strain and tiredness takes its toll. It highlights the need to cast off anything that hinders. Paul speaks of sin that entangles and acts as a distraction.
- The course of any race is marked out. Just so, we can rely on God's guidance and faithfulness, and the example that Jesus has set for us.

I have fought the good fight, I have finished the race, I have kept the faith. (2 Timothy 4:7)

- Paul talks about finishing the race, having run the race fairly and to the best of his ability, and in a way that is honouring to God. I emphasise once again that the race is a metaphor for living out the Christian life whilst here on earth.

So we make it our goal to please him, whether we are at home in the body or away from it. (2 Corinthians 5:9)

- What are your goals in life, i.e. your aims and purpose? Our aim in life should be to please God.

Not that I have already obtained all this, or have already been made perfect, but I press on to take hold of that for which Christ Jesus took hold of me. (Philippians 3:12)

- None of us have reached perfection, but our aims or purpose in life should be to press on towards achieving the things that Jesus has called us to do in his service, and to be the people that he wants us to be.
- Once again, the concept of perseverance is implied here.

Are you so foolish? After beginning with the Spirit are you now trying to attain your goal by human effort?
(Galatians 3:3)

- Our only hope to achieve the goals set for us by God, and to achieve Jesus' calling to service, is through the power of the Holy Spirit working in us, through us and around us.
- We should never give up trusting in divine assistance; if we do, we will fail dramatically.

Again, it will be like a man going on a journey, who called his servants and entrusted his property to them.
(Matthew 25:14)

- God has given us the resources that we need to achieve the work Jesus has set before us. Let's not waste those resources, or the time that he has allocated to us on this earth (Matthew 25:14-30).

Read the rest of this story.

For example
Look at the story of Onesimus in the letter to Philemon. Onesimus, Philemon's slave, runs away. He has never served his master well. However, whilst fleeing, he meets with Paul and becomes a Christian. He is transformed by the experience of meeting with Jesus and being filled with the Holy Spirit, and

it is his desire to return to his old master and be a good slave. Imagine that! It is even possible to glorify God in being a slave. So Onesimus turns from running away, to running the race.

A guide to spirituality for today's young adults
- There is a metaphorical race to be run and goals to be achieved; goals like living out the Christian life of love and witness, following Jesus' example and responding to God's personal calling to you. Take part with perseverance and willingness to do your best.
- The race that you run should be God-centred.
- You will be equipped, guided and empowered to complete the race successfully and meet your goals.
- Never try to run the race or reach the goals in your own strength – if you do, you will certainly fail!
- Waste nothing on the way!

4. LAST BUT NOT LEAST

< PAST – PRESENT – FUTURE >
Before looking at this session, take your notebook and spend a few minutes jotting down some notes about yourself:

- *Are you running the race or running away?*
- *If you are running away, maybe you would prefer to be in the race instead.*
- *Since the last session, have you noticed any of your goals in life changing?*
- *Are you willing to be part of God's plans and purposes now and in the future?*

Ask the questions

- Why did God give us freedom of choice, knowing that we would make so many wrong choices?
- What happens when we make wrong choices?

Introduction

From the moment we wake up in the morning until the moment we go to sleep at night, we are bombarded with one decision after another. Maybe the first choice we face is whether to turn the alarm off, roll over and go to sleep again, or make a move to get up. We have to decide what to wear, to bath or shower, what the breakfast menu will be, etc. Some of the choices we face are merely personal preferences; others are more crucial and some even life changing. There are choices which we make where the wrong decision will have serious, detrimental results. Because we live in a broken world, some of the issues we face are blurred with grey areas – the right decision can lack clarity. Sadly, history seems to prove that, a lot of the time, we're actually not very good at making choices.

Maybe, as you gaze at the car standing in your drive, you think to yourself, 'I wish I had gone for the red one!'

Perhaps as you sit on the bus going to work, you think to yourself, 'I wish I had worked harder at school, so that I could have done something more interesting'.

Have you entered into relationships that you now regret? Are there things in your life that, given the choice again, you wouldn't have done – or missed opportunities that you wish you had taken advantage of?

Are there pockets of wasted time?

Do you get the idea?

What the Bible says

When the woman saw that the fruit of the tree was good for food and pleasing to the eye, and also desirable for gaining wisdom, she took some and ate it. She also gave some to her husband, who was with her, and he ate it. (Genesis 3:6)

- In Genesis 3:1-24, Adam and Eve discover what it means to make the *wrong choice*.
- They choose to disobey God and discover that some of the choices we make have very serious – and even eternal – consequences.

Now Cain said to his brother Abel, 'Let's go out to the field.' And while they were in the field, Cain attacked his brother Abel and killed him. (Genesis 4:8)

- Read also verses 1-7. Something about Cain's offering to God is not right: maybe he chooses to give God second best; maybe he gives the best but chooses to give it with a bad attitude. God offers him the chance to put things right, but Cain chooses not to.

- Cain eventually chooses to kill his brother in a jealous rage – another wrong choice!
- The story of Cain and Abel is a series of wrong choices with catastrophic consequences.
- It is so easy for something like anger or jealousy to set off a chain reaction of wrong decisions in our lives.

The Lord saw how great man's wickedness on earth had become, and that every inclination of the thoughts of his heart was only evil all the time. (Genesis 6:5)

- The situation at the time of Noah is one of people having made the choice to live lives governed by the powers of evil and self-centred desires.
- What do you think God would think about the twenty-first century world?

But the Lord said to Samuel, 'Do not consider his appearance or his height, for I have rejected him. The Lord does not look at the things man looks at. Man looks at the outward appearance, but the Lord looks at the heart.' (1 Samuel 16:7)

- Samuel falls into the trap of basing his decision on outward appearances. God is more interested in what lies within: our thoughts, feelings, motives, beliefs, response to him, etc.
- It is an easy trap to fall into, especially when we are bombarded with advertisements that are based on things like our physical appearance and image building.

Enter through the narrow gate. For wide is the gate and broad is the road that leads to destruction, and many enter through it. But small is the gate and narrow the road that leads to life, and only a few find it. (Matthew 7:13-14)

- Jesus puts a choice before us in this parable to enter through the wide or narrow gates.
- The wide gate is symbolic of living the kind of lifestyle that comes easily, one which indulges our selfish and self-centred desires; a lifestyle that has an incredibly destructive side to it, which is not always apparent in the first instance.
- The narrow gate portrays a difficult lifestyle, following Jesus and living for the good of others, but one which leads to fulfilment and blessing.
- This is a choice that affects the eternal.

Therefore everyone who hears these words of mine and puts them into practice is like a wise man who built his house on the rock. (Matthew 7:24)

- Take a look at the complete parable of Matthew 7:24-27 – a simple story which is blatantly obvious. No one would dream of building a house on the foundation of sand. So, why do people build their lives on values and dynamics that lead to destruction?
- The person who builds on rock (responding positively to Jesus and his teaching) is like those who enter through the narrow gate.
- Jesus emphasises that this is a choice we all have to make at some time in our lives.

So I say, live by the Spirit, and you will not gratify the desires of the sinful nature. (Galatians 5:16)

- See Galatians 5:16-26. In a previous chapter we looked at the fruit of the Spirit. This short passage emphasises once again that how we live our lives is a choice that we make. We can either choose to follow Jesus and be fulfilled, motivated, empowered and guided by the Holy Spirit, or go our own way.

Jesus answered, 'I am the way and the truth and the life. No one comes to the Father except through me.' (John 14:6)

- In this verse Jesus highlights that he is the way: the way to enter into a close relationship with God; the way to leading a fulfilled life (now and eternally); and the way to understand and be empowered by the indwelling Holy Spirit to live according to the truth.

Then he said to them all: 'If anyone would come after me, he must deny himself and take up his cross daily and follow me.' (Luke 9:23)

- Following Jesus is not always an easy way of life, but one that is filled with eternal potential, fulfilment and promise.
- Remember, there are consequences to the choices we make.
- Jesus says, 'Follow me' – you have the choice.

For example
How many examples of people turning to Jesus would you like? The New Testament is full of them!

In Mark 2:13-17, Levi (Matthew) leaves his old way of life behind to follow Jesus. Luke 19:1-10 tells the story of a man who realises that the whole dynamic to his life is wrong and unfulfilling – his life is transformed through meeting with Jesus.

Saul (Paul) certainly *sees the light* in Acts 9:1-19; his whole life is turned around for the better, through responding positively to the call of Jesus.

A guide to spirituality for today's young adults

- God has given us freedom of choice, but in our own wisdom we are not particularly good at making those more important and even life-changing choices.
- Following Jesus in faith results in being filled with the indwelling Holy Spirit. He will guide you in the important choices you have to make.
- Choosing to follow Jesus and live life his way is a choice that has eternal implications.
- Why did God give us freedom of choice, knowing that we would make wrong choices? The reason is simple: so that we could choose to have a close relationship with him through following Jesus in faith.

5. COMFORTABLY OFF

< PAST – PRESENT – FUTURE >
Before looking at this session, take your notebook and spend a few minutes jotting down some notes about yourself:

- *Have you faced any particularly hard choices or decisions since reading the previous chapter? Looking back, do you feel that the choices or decisions you came to were good ones?*
- *After working through the previous chapter, has the way that you approach choosing and making decisions changed in any way? If not, would you like it to change? How?*
- *Looking further back over your life, are there any significant bad choices or decisions that you can now recognise? Can anything be done now to put things right?*
- *What decision have you come to regarding choosing God?*

Ask the questions
- Am I just making excuses?
- Why do I need God?

Introduction
What do you buy the person who seems to have everything that they need or want? It is the same every Christmas – there always seems to be someone on the presents list who is impossible to buy for. I suppose that different people have different views of what makes life comfortable. To some, it would be a good marriage, two children, a mortgage on a three-bedroom house, two cars and a job bringing in a good salary. To others, it might involve being single and having the money and free-

dom to travel. Yet still others appear to find contentment with very little.

During a school assembly some years ago, I asked the question, 'What kind of things do we need?' There were some well thought out answers: food, water, warmth, shelter, love and hope. I wonder what kind of answers would come from a similar survey amongst adults. What do you really need? What would you say leads to contentment? Is it possible to become too comfortable, or so focussed on things we don't really need that, as a result, we miss out on the really important things in life?

What the Bible says

> So God created man in his own image, in the image of God he created him; male and female he created them.
> (Genesis 1:27)

- We're back to being created in God's image. We have been created to be like him, in order to share fellowship with him. There is a space, a void – call it what you will – that can only be filled or satisfied by a close relationship with God.

> Then he said, 'This is what I'll do. I will tear down my barns and build bigger ones, and there I will store all my grain and my goods. And I'll say to myself, "You have plenty of good things laid up for many years. Take life easy; eat, drink and be merry."' (Luke 12:18-19)

- Read on to the end of the story (Luke 12:13-21). In accumulating his material needs and enjoying the transient comfort of wealth, the farmer has missed out on the most important things in life – the things of God.
- When things are going well it is all too easy to become too

comfortable to see the need for God. Suddenly the realisation comes that there has to be more to life than this! Sometimes the realisation comes too late.

- Does that ring any bells? Perhaps someone you know, or maybe even yourself?

At the time of the banquet he sent his servant to tell those who had been invited, 'Come, for everything is now ready.' But they all alike began to make excuses. The first said, 'I have just bought a field, and I must go and see it. Please excuse me.' (Luke 14:17-18)

- It is so easy to make excuses: I don't have time ... I'm too busy ... If it were any other day ...
- As these verses suggest, the parable that they are taken from is all about making excuses. Look at the rest of the parable (Luke 14:15-24). In its deeper meaning, these are not excuses about trivial things. The parable of the Great Banquet is all about choosing to follow Jesus and experience his eternal blessing ... or not!
- Sadly, many people in the twenty-first century don't even seem to bother to make excuses for not pursuing the things of God. Apathy is worse than opposition or resistance.

Here now is the man who did not make God his stronghold but trusted in his great wealth and grew strong by destroying others! (Psalm 52:7)

- It is an easy trap to fall into: gaining riches, power and success in material terms at the expense of others. Profit comes before people. Materialism comes before the things of God.

Have a look at the whole Psalm.

The wealth of the rich is their fortified city; they imagine it an unscalable wall. (Proverbs 18:11)

- It is true that there is a certain security which can be found in wealth and in the physical world in which we live. That is, until things like grief, failing health or death appear. Suddenly the benefits seem to take on a whole new perspective.
- No one has yet succeeded in taking their physical wealth with them on facing death. A different kind of wealth is needed as an investment for eternity.

Command those who are rich in this present world not to be arrogant nor to put their hope in wealth, which is so uncertain, but to put their hope in God, who richly provides us with everything for our enjoyment. (1 Timothy 6:17)

- 1 Timothy 6:17 provides the answer to the dilemma outlined in the previous section.
- Physical wealth is precarious at the best of times: investments can fail; material possessions are susceptible to wear, tear, damage and corrosion; power and success have a tendency to crumble.
- Eternal hope and investment is found only in the things of God, through a close relationship with him, through repentance and faith in Jesus.

Jesus answered, 'I am the way and the truth and the life. No-one comes to the Father except through me.' (John 14:6)

- This discusses the way to a restored relationship with God the Father.
- In word and deed, Jesus demonstrates and teaches the truth about God and his purposes for creation.

- Repentance and faith in Jesus is the only way to be forgiven for the things we do wrong, and thus to live in the hope of spending eternity in the presence and blessing of the Triune God (God the Father, Jesus the Son and Holy Spirit).

For example:
Read Luke 19:1-10. The story of Zacchaeus illustrates so well the whole point of this session. Zacchaeus is a person who has been totally reliant on wealth and the dishonest gain of it. However, he comes to the point of realising that his past lifestyle was shallow and unfulfilling. He decides to make changes before it is too late and meets with Jesus. He repents and commits his life to following Jesus in faith. The change in his life is phenomenal and instant – and eternal!

A guide to spirituality for today's young adults
- You have been created in the image of God, with the intention of you sharing a wonderful and close relationship with the Triune God.
- Beware of becoming too comfortable at the expense of the things of God.
- The things of the physical world in which we live now are transient. The things of God are eternal. It is easy to fall into the trap of focusing on that which does not last.
- Jesus warns us about making excuses for putting off the most important decision we will ever face: whether or not to follow him in faith.
- Zacchaeus is a wonderful example of someone coming to the realisation that things have got to change, and he finds his answer when he meets personally with Jesus. The living Jesus still changes lives for the better.

6. SET FREE

< Past – Present – Future >
Before looking at this session, take your notebook and spend a few minutes jotting down some notes about yourself:

- *Has that void in your life been filled and satisfied with a close relationship with God, through Jesus?*
- *What is your focus in life? Is it the things of God, or material objects?*
- *Have your focus and priorities changed at all since you have begun this journey through scripture?*
- *Are there people who you have made use of in the desire for financial gain, to whom you need to say 'sorry'?*
- *Where does your future hope lay now?*

Ask the questions
- Why do I need to be forgiven?
- How many times am I expected to forgive someone who hurts me?

Introduction
If a balloon is pricked hard enough with something sharp, eventually it will burst. If a bowl of water is tipped upside down, it will make a terrible mess. If a bone china teacup is accidentally dropped from a considerable height onto a hard floor, it will break. If a person steps out onto a busy road, right in front of a large lorry going fifty miles an hour, he or she is not likely to survive. These are all consequences which we have learned about either by personal experience, things we have

observed or knowledge that has been passed on to us. For the same reasons, we know that if we get caught for speeding in our cars, at the very least we will get some kind of warning – or it could be as serious as losing our licence. Other criminal offences carry allotted penalties, maybe even prison sentences. Unfaithfulness in marriage causes all kinds of hurt and damage. It is not quite as alien as many like to believe that our choices and actions do have consequences – some good and some bad – and that we should take responsibility for those consequences. We have all acted on bad choices at times in our lives, causing hurt and pain in our own lives and in the lives of others. At those times the only way to really move forward and be free is by the way of forgiveness.

What the Bible says
> To Adam he said, 'Because you listened to your wife and ate from the tree about which I commanded you, "You must not eat of it ..."' (Genesis 3:17a)

- Have a look at the whole of Genesis 3:1-24. It says that when we are disobedient to God (sin), there will be consequences – serious ones.
- Those consequences are things like pain, suffering, fear, shame, physical death and separation from God.
- Some of the consequences of sin we experience as a result of our own sin, the sin of others and also as a result of living in a world that has been damaged by sin through the ages.

> For all have sinned and fall short of the glory of God, and are justified freely by his grace through the redemption that came by Christ Jesus. (Romans 3:23-24)

- The reality is that we have all fallen short of God's standards and expectations of us. Therefore, we all face the consequences of sin. The good news is that through repentance and faith in Jesus, we can be forgiven and restored in our relationship with God. We will then be set free from those consequences; in part now, but in full when Jesus returns (Acts 1:11).
- Redemption means that the prices or penalties for the wrong things we have done have been paid in full – through Jesus' death on the cross.

Just as the Son of Man did not come to be served, but to serve, and to give his life as a ransom for many. (Matthew 20:28)

- Read the account of the crucifixion of Jesus in Luke 23:26-56. Take particular note of the verses concerning the two criminals (Luke 23:39-43). A ransom is paid to set someone free from captivity. Jesus' death on the cross pays the price for humankind to be set free from sin's consequences; through repentance and faith in him we are forgiven.

He himself bore our sins in his body on the tree, so that we might die to sins and live for righteousness; by his wounds you have been healed. (1 Peter 2:24)

- One of sin's consequences is physical death. In love, Jesus takes our sins upon himself as he dies on the cross. Through his selfless act both love and justice are satisfied.

Jesus said to her, 'I am the resurrection and the life. He who believes in me will live, even though he dies.' (John 11:25)

- Jesus promises that those who believe – in other words, those who follow him in faith, and have been forgiven and restored – will receive eternal life (See Isaiah 25:6-8).

Then Peter came to Jesus and asked, 'Lord, how many times shall I forgive my brother when he sins against me? Up to seven times?' Jesus answered, 'I tell you, not seven times, but seventy-seven times.' (Matthew 18:21-22)

- From being forgiven, we move on to the topic of forgiving others who have done things to hurt us. Jesus' reply to Peter's question suggests that we should go on forgiving as many times as is necessary.

Forgive us our debts, as we also have forgiven our debtors. (Matthew 6:12)

- The prayer that Jesus teaches us in Matthew 6:9-13 draws an inseparable link between being forgiven by God, and forgiving others when they hurt us in some way.

Read the rest of the prayer.

For example

In Mark 2:1-12 we read about a paralysed man who is lowered through a hole in the roof in order to get to Jesus, because of the huge crowd. Obviously the intentions of his friends were that Jesus would heal him. Everyone is surprised when he says the words, 'Your sins are forgiven'. Jesus does go on to heal him, but in the process he is highlighting the need and importance of spiritual healing or forgiveness.

A guide to spirituality for today's young adults

- It is part of everyday life that actions have consequences.
- Sin or disobedience to God has very serious consequences.
- The bad news is that everyone has sinned. The good news is that through repentance and faith in Jesus, all of humankind can be set free from the consequences, in part now, and in full when Jesus returns.
- On the cross Jesus has paid the penalty for our sin.
- Through the resurrected Jesus, his followers can be sure of eternal life in all its fullness.
- When you receive God's forgiveness through repentance and faith in Jesus, you should go on to forgive those who hurt you.

7. IN THE LION'S DEN

< PAST – PRESENT – FUTURE >
Before looking at this session, take your notebook and spend a few minutes jotting down some notes about yourself:

- *Is there someone who you need to forgive, because they have hurt you in some way in the past? Are you going to forgive them?*
- *Have you accepted the forgiveness that God offers to you through repentance and faith in Jesus?*
- *Do you feel confident that you will enjoy eternal life in the presence of the Triune God?*

Ask the questions
- What is expected from Christian people today?
- Love and respect: who cares?

Introduction
We live in a world where expectations come from many different angles: family, work, the State, peers, society and God. I wonder what society's expectations are of the Church. People still seem to expect it to be there for the usual marriages, births and deaths, even if many rarely set foot inside the building in between times. Could there be some disappointment that the modern Church no longer appears to be making such a strong stand on a variety of issues?

In reality people like to have some kind of boundaries and guidelines to work towards; when these guidelines are not present a type of void or emptiness opens up – perhaps even a feeling of being let down or uncared for. We need to remember that the Church is not buildings or traditions, it is people. So what do people look for in the lives of those who profess to be Christians? Some perhaps think that Christians are 'holier than thou' and judgemental – that should not be the case. Others may see Christianity as being irrelevant and out of date – but of course, it is timeless. And there are those whose expectations are of someone who strives to live according to a set of values that society constantly seems to be eroding – thus highlighting how important a witnessing lifestyle is.

What are God's expectations of the Church – that is, Jesus' followers? In a society that is changing so quickly and in so many different ways, we need wisdom as we apply the Scriptures to everyday situations. In a world that has been damaged by sin, those ever increasing *grey areas* can be difficult to deal with. This chapter is not called 'In the Lion's Den' for nothing!

What the Bible says

> So the king gave the order, and they brought Daniel and threw him into the lion's den. The king said to Daniel, 'May your God, whom you serve continually, rescue you!' (Daniel 6:16)

- Have a look at the whole of the chapter. Daniel *literally* faces the lion's den, because of his refusal to be prevented from doing what he knows to be right. Sometimes as we live life in a twenty-first century society, we feel as if we are *metaphorically* facing the lion's den time and time again as we try to do *the right thing*.
- Doing *the right thing* is often met with varying degrees of opposition, like peer pressure or society's falling standards.

> '*You are the salt of the earth ... You are the light of the world ...*' (Matthew 5:13a, 14a)

- Have a look at Matthew 5:13-16. Jesus tells his followers to be salt and light. In other words, to make a positive difference in the world.
- Salt adds flavour, preserves and has abrasive qualities. Being a Christian involves sharing with others the flavours of the joy, peace and hope that come from a close relationship with Jesus. There is a responsibility to provide a good example of morality to society. And at times, in order to make a stand, it is necessary to be abrasive – go against the flow!
- Light, of course, shows the way and reveals things hidden in the darkness. In sharing the message of Scripture we can pass on the truth that Jesus brings; a truth which shows the way and reveals the things that are not of God (John 14:6).

Do not think that I have come to abolish the law or the Prophets; I have not come to abolish them but to fulfil them. (Matthew 5:17)

- The commandments are an expression of God's love for us. They help us to show love and respect to others.
- Jesus explains that he has not come to do away with the commandments but to explain them in greater detail, and help us to understand their significance and application.

You have heard that it was said, 'Do not commit adultery.' But I tell you that anyone who looks at a woman lustfully has already committed adultery with her in his heart. (Matthew 5:27-28)

- Jesus goes on to demonstrate how the commandments of the Old Testament can be expanded, so that their significance is far greater than we might imagine.

- He explains in Matthew 5:27-28 that it is not just committing the act of adultery that is against the seventh commandment, but also things like lustful thoughts and fantasies.

  You shall not murder. You shall not steal. You shall not give false testimony against your neighbour. (Exodus 20:13, 15-16)

Try expanding the Ten Commandments, for example:

- Murder in the sixth commandment is the extreme, but it can be expanded to say that we shouldn't deliberately cause physical or mental harm of any kind to others. In fact, we should endeavour to do good at all times.
- The eighth can be widened beyond stealing physical possessions. Think about stealing time from God and others, sharing confidences that are not ours to share, and so on.
- The ninth could be interpreted as much more than just not telling lies about neighbours; it is about being truthful in all things. That includes not telling lies, not telling half-truths and not misleading others by keeping quiet about the truth.

  Now you are the body of Christ, and each one of you is a part of it. (1 Corinthians 12:27)

- As I said earlier, it is always important to remember that when we talk about the Christian Church, we are talking about the people and not the buildings. When a person commits to following Jesus in repentance and with faith, he or she becomes part of the Church.
- The body of Christ is a way in which Jesus illustrates what the Church is like: a body of people, all followers of Jesus committed to continuing his work here on earth; differ-

ent people, with different characteristics, gifts and abilities; people called to a variety of different tasks, but all equally as important.

- We must always remember that the body is controlled by the head. In the case of this illustration the head is Jesus himself, to who we should always be looking for guidance and example.

At that time the kingdom of heaven will be like ten virgins who took their lamps and went out to meet the bridegroom. Five of them were foolish and five were wise. (Matthew 25:1-2)

- Read the whole parable in Matthew 25:1-13. The ten virgins represent those who profess to be Christians. The parable says that the harsh reality is that not all those who say they are Christians really are.
- The difference between the wise and foolish virgins is that the former have remembered to prepare for the wait at the wedding feast by bringing spare oil. The oil represents the lifestyle evidence of those who are really committed to Jesus and doing his work.

You see that his faith and his actions were working together, and his faith was made complete by what he did. (James 2:22)

- Read James 2:14-22. The lifestyle that we live is not only the evidence of our faith in Jesus, but it is also the thing that gives our witness authenticity to other people.

For example
The life of Jesus on earth is our perfect example of how to live the Christian life of love and witness. Look through the shortest gospel – the Gospel of Mark – and see for yourself.

A guide to spirituality for today's young adults

- Societies expectations of the Christian Church, and thus the people of God, are probably quite varied, distorted and in many ways not the same as God's.
- Living as a Christian in the world today can be like being in a metaphorical lion's den. It is not easy to stand up for God's values. There will be times when you feel under attack from all directions.
- Christians are called to be salt and light to the world. God wants you to make a difference!
- The commandments are an expression of God's love; as such they are for the good of all his creation. They help us to love and respect each other. They do still apply nowadays, especially when they are understood in all their fullness.
- Christians are part of the body of Christ, with important tasks to perform, uniquely empowered and gifted, and all equally important.
- The evidence of whether or not you are a follower of Jesus will be through the lifestyle you lead; there is the strength of your witness.

8. FACING THE HEAT

< PAST – PRESENT – FUTURE >

Before looking at this session, take your notebook and spend a few minutes jotting down some notes about yourself:

- *How did you find session seven? Did it give you any causes for concern about your own lifestyle? Are there any regrets regarding your past? What are you going to do about it?*
- *How do you think other people see you? Do they see something of Jesus shining out?*
- *Are you willing to be part of the body of Christ?*
- *Will you let the Holy Spirit work in you, to enable you to be the person God wants you to be, and say and do the things he wants you to say and do?*
- *Have your future hopes, dreams or expectations changed since writing your first entry for < Past – Present – Future >? If so, how?*

Ask the questions
- Who should I listen to?
- What are idols?

Introduction
Next time you watch a dog or cat getting ready to go to sleep, observe their endeavours to get comfortable. They look for just the right place: somewhere warm, a place in the sunshine or near the fire, preferably soft and quiet. And then, before lying down, they will claw at the cushions, carpet or blankets, and maybe turn round and round in endless circles before settling

down, ready for a sleep. Maybe *you* puff up the cushions or pillow before settling down yourself. Perhaps you like a hot water bottle or electric blanket. Possibly you have a particular way in which you like to have the duvet over you: wrapping yourself up, feet poking out of the bottom. *We*, like our pets, enjoy being comfortable. Yet becoming comfortable in the Christian life can lead to laziness, apathy or complacency. Laziness, apathy and complacency can lead to a willingness to conform – anything for a quiet life! And, indeed, there are all too many pressures to conform in the modern world. Peer pressure comes in many different forms and age groups: at school, in the workplace, part of family life, pressure from the neighbourhood and society in general, as well as from the world of advertising. Advice comes in many different forms and then confusion steps in. Who should we listen to? When does conformity to the pressures of society lead to worshipping modern idols?

What the Bible says:

> *'You will not surely die,' the serpent said to the woman. 'For God knows that when you eat of it your eyes will be opened, and you will be like God, knowing good and evil.'*
> *(Genesis 3:4-5)*

- The complete story of Adam and Eve is found in Genesis 3:1-24. From the beginning of time, the devil has given bad advice; and today it comes to us in many different forms and disguises, playing on our human desires, weaknesses and judgement.

> *Now when you hear the sound of the horn, flute, zither, lyre, harp, pipes and all kind of music, if you are ready to fall down and worship the image I made, very good. But if you do not*

worship it, you will be thrown immediately into a blazing furnace. Then what god will be able to rescue you from my hand? (Daniel 3:15)

- Read the rest of the story about Meshach, Shadrach and Abednego (Daniel 3:1-30). The three young men are under tremendous pressure to conform to the king's demands. If they refuse, they will risk being burned alive in a fiery furnace. Standing up for God's standards, against the majority and the powerful, can result in consequences ranging from abuse to threats of violence or being ostracised, to something even worse.
- Meshach, Shadrach and Abednego could easily have conformed to the king's decree and worshipped the idol built of gold. But that would have meant letting God down and resulted in living a life of guilt. At least by refusing to comply their consciences will be at peace. They know that God is able to save them, but they accept that he may not chose to do so, for some reason known only to himself.
- We may not worship golden statues in the modern western world, but there are all sorts of other things that fall into the category of idols: money, possessions, power, fame, immoral lifestyles and addictions.
- It takes courage to make a stand for what is right. Peer pressure is very strong. Sometimes it means protesting against government legislation. It can leave us isolated and even ostracised.

When Jesus heard this, he said to him, 'You still lack one thing. Sell everything that you have and give to the poor, and you will have treasure in heaven. Then come, follow me.' When he heard this, he became very sad, because he was a man of great wealth. (Luke 18:22-23)

- Read the whole story, which can be found in Luke 18:18-30. Having money in itself isn't wrong, but the temptation is to begin to worship it, making it into an idol – the idol of materialism, the idol of greed, the idol of selfishness.

- The man in the story is guilty of the love of money and selfishness, hence Jesus not only tells him to get rid of his money, but he is to use it to help the poor.

He also saw a poor widow put in two very small copper coins. 'I tell you the truth,' he said, 'this poor widow has put in more than all the others.' (Luke 21:2-3)

- As Jesus and his disciples stand near the offering boxes outside the temple, they notice a poor widow putting in two small copper coins – worth very little. Others throw handfuls of valuable coins in. Imagine the surprise of Jesus' disciples at his remark. How could her gift have been more than all the others? It's all about proportions. The widow gave all that she had to live on; others were just giving a small percentage of their wealth.

- This story is about focus and priorities. It speaks about where our focus lies. And of course it goes beyond just money: how do we use our possessions, time and abilities? Where is the focus of our worship?

For example
Before Jesus' ministry begins, the devil tempts him in the desert (Matthew 4:1-11). 'You could be Mr Popular,' he taunts, 'just satisfy their selfish desires and they'll follow you.' Jesus turns to the teaching of scripture and refuses to follow the devil's advice. During his ministry, Jesus is never afraid to stand up to those who promote evil, self-centredness, deceit and hypocrisy. He is never afraid to tell the truth about the

Kingdom. Needless to say, Jesus is very unpopular with many (see Luke 20:46-47).

A guide to spirituality for today's young adults

- There are many sources of advice, but few of them are truly helpful and in accordance with God's will and values. Remember the devil appears in many different guises in the modern world.
- Prayer is needed to discern who to take advice from.
- Jesus sets the example of courage, truthfulness and looking to Scripture for answers.
- Conformity may appear to be the easy way out, but it comes with all kinds of serious consequences.
- Standing up for what is right can be very costly in many different ways, but the influence for good can be immense – as is God's ultimate blessing.
- Getting your priorities right is essential. Remember the Triune God should always be first in your life.
- Putting God first sometimes means letting go of other things; the kind of things that are incompatible.

9. MEETING WITH GIANTS

< Past – Present – Future >
Before looking at this session, take your notebook and spend a few minutes jotting down some notes about yourself:

- Did the last session make you think about to whom or where you look for advice? What conclusions have you come to, and how do you expect that to change your life?
- What kind of issues are you faced with, for example, at work, in the family and socially? What are your views about them? Would you be prepared to make a stand for what you believe to be right?
- Have your priorities changed since reading chapter eight? In what ways have they changed?
- Are there things in your life that are not compatible with the things of God? What are they and what do you intend to do about them? (It could be something in the past that needs putting right.)

Ask the question
- What should I do in a crisis?

Introduction
There are situations we must face from time to time that just seem to swamp us with their enormity. Though they can be varied in type, they still have a tendency to leave us staggering. Let me give some examples: serious illness, bereavement, redundancy, fear, loneliness, guilt, shame, discouragement, worry, feelings of hopelessness, debt, natural disasters, and so

on. How can we get by at these times, especially when others are relying on us to be strong for them? We have to be careful that when coming up with a coping strategy we do not belittle the severity, impact and struggle of dealing with such times.

What the Bible says

A champion named Goliath, who was from Gath, came out of the Philistines' camp. He was over nine feet tall.
(1 Samuel 17:4)

Saul replied, 'You are not able to go out against this Philistine and fight him; you are only a boy, and he has been a fighting man from his youth.' (1 Samuel 17:33)

'The Lord who delivered me from the paw of the lion and the paw of the bear will deliver me from the hand of this Philistine.' Saul said to David, 'Go, and the Lord be with you.' (1 Samuel 17:37)

- Read the whole story of David and Goliath (1 Samuel 17:1-58). You would not want to get on the wrong side of Goliath, standing at over nine feet high. The Israelite soldiers are scared to take him on, but not young David. What is David's secret? Where does his courage come from?
- David places his full trust in the strength of God, basing it on his faithfulness to him in the past.
- Whatever the 'giants' we face might be, God can help.

I am the Lord your God, who brought you out of Egypt, out of the land of slavery. (Exodus 20:2)

- On a number of occasions in the Old Testament, God reminds the Israelites of his faithfulness to them in the past.

- It is good to look back at God's faithfulness in the past to encourage us as we face present difficulties and hardships.
- The nature and faithfulness of God is unchanging – on that we can depend!

Going a little farther, he fell with his face to the ground and prayed, 'My father, if it is possible, may this cup be taken from me. Yet not as I will, but as you will.' (Matthew 26:39)

Your kingdom come,
Your will be done
On earth as it is in heaven. (Matthew 6:10)

- As Jesus faces a horrendous death on the cross, he is able to pray to the Father: 'Yet not as I will, but as you will.'
- The word's of the prayer that Jesus taught are 'your will be done'.
- The whole issue of suffering is a hard one to understand. Certainly God doesn't instigate suffering (as demonstrated in the book of Job), but there are times when he allows suffering for a reason. The trouble is twofold: firstly, that we often don't understand his reasons; and secondly, in the midst of suffering it is not easy to look for the positive. It can be very hard to reach the point of praying that God's will be done.

I am not saying this because I am in need, for I have learned to be content in whatever the circumstances.
(Philippians 4:11)

- Paul has found the secret of contentment. Our modern society in many ways promotes discontentment, particularly in materialistic ways as we are encouraged to buy that which we don't really want, and more importantly, don't need.

- Discontentment must raise stress and anxiety levels, and thus ends up having negative effects on health and feelings of wellbeing.
- Could it also make us less accepting of negative happenings in our lives?

The one who received the seed that fell among the thorns is the man who hears the word, but the worries of this life and the deceitfulness of wealth choke it, making it unfruitful. (Matthew 13:22)

- Jesus tells us not to worry unduly about things. That is not to say that we shouldn't take responsibility and use common sense, but our primary focus in life should not be on material things like food and clothes, as necessary as they are.

Come to me, all you who are weary and burdened, and I will give you rest. Take my yoke upon you and learn from me, for I am gentle and humble in heart, and you will find rest for your souls. For my yoke is easy and my burden is light. (Matthew 11:28-30)

- There are times when most of us feel weary and burdened, sometimes by quite ordinary, day-to-day routines; sometimes by problems, struggles and hardships.
- Jesus offers to help us bear the burden, if we allow him to. The thought of rest during those occasions of fatigue and strain is a very comforting one.
- There is something about doing things for Jesus that actually relieves the burden, weariness and oppression.
- This passage is just one of many in the Bible that bring

tremendous encouragement to the hurting, weary and downhearted.

For example
- Let's not play down the horrendous cruelty involved with the crucifixion of Jesus (Matthew 27:11-56). He is brutally flogged, a crown of thorns is pressed down onto his head so that the thorns dig into his scalp, he has to carry his own cross and then nails are driven through his flesh before being raised up on the cross to die: 'Yet not as I will, but as you will.'

A guide to spirituality for today's young adults
- When facing metaphorical giants, remember: God is only a prayer away. He can help.
- God is unchanging. He was faithful in the past, is faithful in the present and will be faithful in the future.
- Strive to reach the point of seeking God's will in all things.
- Seek contentment and try not to worry unduly.
- Share the burden with Jesus – it will make the load easier to bear.
- Be encouraged by inspirational passages of Scripture.

10. GROWTH AND MATURITY

< PAST – PRESENT – FUTURE >
Before looking at this session, take your notebook and spend a few minutes jotting down some notes about yourself:

- *Did chapter nine encourage you to think about God's faithfulness to you in the past? If so, what situations came to mind?*
- *Have you spoken to anyone since then who has shared with you something of their experience of God's faithfulness? How did that make you feel?*
- *What kind of things do you worry about?*
- *In what ways could you be described as being discontented?*
- *If your attitude to Scripture has changed, how has it?*
- *Are you facing any metaphorical giants in your life at the moment? What are they and how do you plan to deal with them?*

Ask the question
- What next?

Introduction
We live in a world where so many things seem to be short term. It is a rarity these days for someone to work for the same company from leaving school or college to retirement. The high divorce rate means that we no longer see so many silver or golden wedding anniversaries. The ease of travel today means that fewer people live the whole of their lives in the same village, town, city, or even country. In fact, the numbers of people who emigrate to settle down in another country also seems

to be on the increase. Having said that, we are led to believe that, these days, in many countries people are living longer lives due to medical advances, etc. Old age is a concept that we are becoming increasingly familiar with, and having to adapt to and provide for. Entering into the Christian life is not a fad; it is not 'short term' but an eternal commitment, which involves striving for growth and maturity. Our life here on earth is part of that learning and growing process.

The excitement gained from purchasing a new car, going on an expensive holiday or gaining a promotion at work is often transient. The novelty soon becomes the mundane; the new-ness becomes aged and worn; the joy is forgotten. But there are things that last.

What the Bible says

> But God said to him, 'You fool! This very night your life will be demanded from you. Then who will get what you have pre-pared for yourself?' This is how it will be with anyone who stores up things for himself but is not rich toward God. (Luke 12:20-21)

- These two verses are the climax of one of Jesus' parables, highlighting the futility of accumulating vast amounts of earthly wealth. At the same time they point out that there is an alternative.
- The things of God have an eternal perspective to them, which we can be part of. However, that means turning from a materialistic way of life to one that centres on fol-lowing Jesus.

Remember this parable from chapter five (Luke 12:13-21).

> Yet I hold this against you: you have forsaken your first love. (Revelation 2:4)

- In verse four of the letter to the church in Ephesus (Revelation 2:1-7), the members are accused of losing their first love. To put it plainly, the initial joy and excitement of becoming a Christian has worn off. They have become stale and complacent.
- We can learn a great lesson from this: as our faith grows and develops, we still need to hold onto something of the initial enthusiasm and joy that we experienced on first meeting with Jesus – especially the eagerness to tell others.
- A lot can be learned from many new Christians as they enthusiastically broadcast their faith to others, delve into the Scriptures eagerly and have a desire to change the world for the better.

They devoted themselves to the apostles' teaching and to the fellowship, to the breaking of bread and prayer. (Acts 2:42)

- Read the rest of Acts 2:42-47. It highlights the importance of and the ingredients necessary for Christians or 'believers' to be fed spiritually, in order to grow and mature.
- It particularly speaks to us of commitment. The early Christians or believers demonstrate something of what it means to put God first. Today, there is a temptation for us to yield to the distractions of the modern world in which we live, all too easily.
- If we want to grow and mature in our faith – and be part of a growing fellowship – we need to be committed to prayer: studying scripture, sharing communion together, engaging in a fellowship with God and other Christians – and we need faith and belief.

Pray continually. (1 Thessalonians 5:17)

- This verse emphasises the importance of praying earnestly and regularly.
- Prayer is not a last resort; it should be a first resort. We should take everything to God in prayer: the things that we do and say, our homes and families, our jobs, our neighbourhoods, our church fellowships and the different relationships in our lives.

Since they could not get him to Jesus because of the crowd, they made an opening in the roof above Jesus and, after digging through it, lowered the mat the paralysed man was lying on. (Mark 2:4)

- We looked at this story earlier on, and what a wonderful story of determination, persistence, imagination, resourcefulness, compassionate love and faith this is.
- It is an example of how we should not allow anything to stand between Jesus and us!

And we, who with unveiled faces all reflect the Lord's glory, are being transformed into his likeness with ever-increasing glory, which comes from the Lord, who is the Spirit. (2 Corinthians 3:18)

- This is what Christians should be striving towards. Growth and maturity is all about becoming more like Jesus – no more and no less!

Fathers, do not exasperate your children; instead, bring them up in the training and instruction of the Lord. (Ephesians 6:4)

- Paul, in his letter to the Ephesians, talks about bringing up children in the ways of God; in other words, the vital importance of passing on the truths of the Christian faith to the next generation.

For example
Take a look at Peter's journey of faith: his ups and downs and his perseverance and determination. In Matthew 14:22-33, Peter sinks as he tries to walk on water, but he does step out of the boat in faith. Matthew 26:69-75 describes the way in which Peter denies Jesus, but at least he is there; the others have scattered. Acts 2:41 is confirmation that the Spirit-filled Peter is a very different Peter to the one who sank and the one who claimed no knowledge of Jesus. What a response to his sermon!

A guide to spirituality for today's young adults
- If you are not moving forwards in your faith, you are probably drifting back.
- The Christian faith demands growth towards maturity, i.e. becoming more like Jesus.
- The growth process begins with repentance and faith in Jesus, and continues with things like commitment, prayer, Bible study and teaching, sharing fellowship with God and other Christians, and sharing communion.
- We should then pass on something of the truths of the Christian faith to the next generation.

11. WHAT ABOUT THE HOLY SPIRIT?

< PAST – PRESENT – FUTURE >
Before looking at this session, take your notebook and spend a few minutes jotting down some notes about yourself:

- As you look back, are you growing in your Christian faith? Think particularly about your relationship with the Triune God.
- Do you feel that you have grown as a result of this journey through Scripture?
- Have there been any changes in your attitude to prayer and Bible study?
- What changes would you like to make to your Christian walk?
- How are you at passing on the message of Jesus to others?

Ask the questions
- Who is the Holy Spirit?
- What does the Holy Spirit do?
- What are spiritual gifts?

Introduction
Mobile telephones have transformed modern society in a number of different ways – not necessarily all good. They disrupt meetings, family life, public performances and travel. However, in a society where there is the increasing threat of violence, abuse and crime, mobile telephones are lifelines to many. The availability of people, thanks to these modern gadg-

ets, has meant that business can be conducted more or less anywhere at any time. I have very mixed feelings about the benefits of that, but, I have to admit, it never ceases to amuse me seeing and hearing people walking along the street apparently talking to themselves; but they're not – suddenly the tell-tale earpiece comes into view!

What could have all the advantages of the mobile telephone, but without the disadvantages? A 24/7 eternal link with God himself. One which not only provides communication, but also love, forgiveness, guidance, power and more! And the service is provided free of charge.

What the Bible says

> *In the beginning God created the heavens and the earth. Now the earth was formless and empty, darkness was over the surface of the deep, and the Spirit of God was hovering over the waters. (Genesis 1:1-2)*

- Some people think that the Holy Spirit is not mentioned until the second chapter of Acts, at Pentecost. Not so. In the second verse of scripture comes the first reference to the Holy Spirit being involved in creation.
- The Holy Spirit is part of the Triune God.

> *Then the Lord said to Moses, 'See I have chosen Bezalel son of Uri, the son of Hur, of the tribe of Judah, and I have filled him with the Spirit of God, with skill, ability and knowledge in all kinds of crafts.' (Exodus 31:1-3)*

- The Gifts of the Spirit are abilities given by the Holy Spirit for a particular purpose and to bring blessing and encouragement to others.
- In this verse we see that these abilities are not just spiritual ones like teaching, prophecy and speaking in

tongues. In this case, the gifting involves expertise in a variety of practical crafts.

But when they cried out to the Lord, he raised up for them a deliverer, Othniel son of Kenaz, Caleb's younger brother, who saved them. The Spirit of the Lord came upon him, so that he became Israel's judge and went to war. The Lord gave Cushan-Rishathaim king of Aram into the hands of Othniel, who overpowered him. (Judges 3:9-10)

- This time, the Holy Spirit equips Othniel with a variety of leadership skills, including leading an army into battle.

Then Peter stood up with the Eleven, raised his voice and addressed the crowd. (Acts 2:14a)

- Peter speaks boldly and confidently to the huge crowd, after he has been filled with the Holy Spirit at Pentecost.

There are different kinds of gifts, but the same Spirit. (1 Corinthians 12:4)

- Read the whole of chapter twelve. There are many different gifts of the Spirit, like practical skills, teaching, prophecy and speaking in tongues. Different people receive different gifts to be used to encourage and build up others.
- The Holy Spirit can bless natural abilities and talents when they are offered to Jesus in service.

This is how the birth of Jesus Christ came about: his mother Mary was pledged to be married to Joseph, but before they came together, she was found to be with child through the Holy Spirit. (Matthew 1:18)

- Through the Holy Spirit the miracle of the virgin birth takes place.

  As soon as Jesus was baptised, he went up out of the water. At that moment heaven was opened, and he saw the Spirit of God descending like a dove and lighting on him. (Matthew 3:16)

- In preparation for his ministry, the Holy Spirit comes upon Jesus, equipping him for all that lies ahead.

  They saw what seemed to be tongues of fire that separated and came to rest on each of them. All of them were filled with the Holy Spirit and began to speak in other tongues as the Spirit enabled them. (Acts 2:3-4)

- The difference from the time of Pentecost is that the indwelling Holy Spirit becomes available to all who follow Jesus in faith and with repentance – not just few people, for particular tasks.
- The Holy Spirit provides practical skills, special spiritual abilities, and equips them for ministry and fulfilment of calling.

  But you will receive power when the Holy Spirit comes on you; and you will be my witnesses in Jerusalem, and in all Judea and Samaria, and to the ends of the earth. (Acts 1:8)

- With the calling comes the equipping.

  Peter replied, 'Repent and be baptised, every one of you, in the name of Jesus Christ for the forgiveness of your sins. And you will receive the gift of the Holy Spirit.' (Acts 2:38)

- Peter states in this verse that when we repent and follow Jesus in faith we will receive the Holy Spirit.
- To what extent we are able to benefit from the power of the indwelling Holy Spirit depends on how much freedom we choose to allow him in our lives.

And we, who with unveiled faces all reflect the Lord's glory, are being transformed into his likeness with ever increasing glory, which comes from the Lord, who is the Spirit.
(2 Corinthians 3:18)

- This is a wonderful promise that the Holy Spirit progressively transforms each of Jesus' followers' lives – transforming them into the likeness of Christ himself.

But the fruit of the Spirit is love, joy, peace, patience, kindness, goodness, faithfulness, gentleness and self-control.
(Galatians 5:22-23a)

- As we are transformed more so into the likeness of Christ himself, so we begin to demonstrate more of his characteristics in our lives: the fruit of the Spirit.
- It is important to remember that the fruit of the Spirit is not a self-selection process. We are called to demonstrate all of the fruit in our lives.

For example
Look to the life of Jesus in the gospels. See what it says in Acts: how God anointed Jesus of Nazareth with the Holy Spirit and power, and how he went around doing good and healing all who were under the power of the devil, because God was with him. (Acts 10:38)

A guide to spirituality for today's young adults

- Gifts of the Spirit come in many different forms and for many different purposes: practical and spiritual; short term and long term; some people have one, some another ...
- The Holy Spirit is the power of miracles.
- After Pentecost, the Holy Spirit is God's gift to all to repent and follow Jesus in faith. He transforms, empowers and guides.
- The Holy Spirit will enable you to demonstrate the fruit of the Spirit in your life; to be the person God created you to be.
- Jesus' life on earth is your example of a perfect Spirit-filled life.

APPENDIX

Chapter 1 – What's it all About?

Almighty God,
Thank you that, despite your greatness, you want to communicate with me.

The Bible is not only inspired by you, but it becomes your living word through the truth and unfailing nature of your promises, in the power of the Holy Spirit and by faith in Jesus.

The Scriptures teach me more about you: they unfold your desire to include me in your great eternal plan for creation; through them I learn about Jesus and his offer of freedom, peace and hope; and in them I discover purpose, guidance and boundaries.

Thank you for the Bible – grant me the desire to read it and the understanding and strength to apply it to my life.

Bring your word to life in my life.

In Jesus' name. Amen.

Chapter 2 – The Family Resemblance

Creator God,
Lovingly you have created humankind in your image, giving sovereignty over the other living creatures, providing creative abilities, enabling love to be given and received, and providing a conscience, giving an inner sense of morality. And yet, you have still given me a wonderful quality of uniqueness.

Even though that image has been damaged by sin coming into the world, I thank you that you haven't given up on me, but you sent your son Jesus to reveal yourself to me and provide the way for me to be restored – through faith in him.

Thank you for the enabling power of the Holy Spirit to overcome my human weaknesses and take on your heavenly resemblance.

Help me to strive constantly to be more like you, and to say and do the things that you would have me say and do, and forgive me for the times when I fail to achieve that.

In Jesus' name. Amen.

Chapter 3 – Are you Running the Race or Running Away?

Gracious God,
You have chosen to include me in your plans and purposes.

Thank you for the privilege of service, for the example of Jesus and for the equipping and guidance of the Holy Spirit. Grant me the willingness to be involved in the things you set before me.

As I visualise living out the Christian life of love and witness, and fulfilling the specific tasks you call me to achieve in terms of running a race and reaching goals, give me the focus, perseverance and determination I need to finish. Help me to keep my eyes fixed on the ribbon and my mind set on the prize – enabling me to take seriously the challenge that lies ahead.

In all things may I seek to please you and further the plans for your kingdom.

In Jesus' name. Amen.

Chapter 4 – Last but not Least

Loving God,
You chose to create me in such a way to allow me the freedom to choose and make decisions.

Thank you that in your love and generosity you gave me freedom of choice, so I could ultimately choose to be part of your family, through following Jesus in faith.

Thank you for the joy of making those simple choices like what I eat and what I wear, and for the guidance of the Holy Spirit with the more difficult and life-changing choices and decisions I have to make.

Thank you for your forgiveness when I get it wrong, through repentance and faith in Jesus, and for fresh starts and the opportunity to try again.

Grant me wisdom on those occasions when I am faced with choosing and making decisions, so that I might further your kingdom and be assured of eternal hope.

In Jesus' name. Amen.

Chapter 5 – Comfortably Off

Creator God,
Thank you that in your love you created me to be like you, with the desire to share fellowship with me eternally.

Thank you that in your love you allowed me to have freedom of choice, so that I might choose you.

Thank you that though the things of the physical world in which I live get damaged and wear out, including my human body, when I follow Jesus with repentance and in faith I have an eternal hope, which includes wonderful blessing and wholeness.

Increase my faith.

Fill me with the desire to spend time with you in prayer and Bible study.
Help me and others to make the right choices and not to give you any excuses.
In Jesus' name. Amen.

Chapter 6 – Set Free

God of forgiveness,
You are the God of salvation: longing to forgive and set all humankind free from the consequences of sin.
Thank you for allowing Jesus to give his life on the cross for everyone, paying the penalty for sin – that includes me.
Thank you that he rose again and is alive today, so that through repentance and faith in him I can be sure of forgiveness, restoration in my relationship with you and eternal life in your presence.
Forgive me for the times when I have disobeyed you and fallen short of your expectations.
Strengthen and guide me as I seek to live a better life in the future and be more like Jesus himself.
Help me to forgive others who have done things to hurt or upset me.
Be in my relationships with others, especially those with whom I struggle.
Let there be more forgiveness in the world today.
In Jesus' name. Amen.

Chapter 7 – In the Lion's Den

Almighty God,
Thank you for the teaching of scripture and the example of Jesus, both of which tell me how to live out the Christian life of love and witness.

Thank you for all your commandments, which you have given to us all for our own good and that of the whole of creation.

Grant me the wisdom, empowerment and understanding to unwrap and apply those commandments to my daily living.

Thank you that there is a unique and special task for me to perform as part of the body of Christ, for which I will be equipped through the power of the Holy Spirit – if I am willing.

Help me to lead the kind of lifestyle that will evidence my faith in Jesus.

Grant me your strength and protection during those times when it is difficult to stand up for what is right.

In Jesus' name. Amen.

Chapter 8 – Facing the Heat

God of all truthfulness,
Thank you for the example of Meshach, Shadrach and Abednego; for their refusal to worship idols, courage in standing up for what is right and willingness to place their future into your powerful hands.

Thank you for the example of Jesus in putting your kingdom before the desire to be popular, and to look to the Scriptures to find the answers to difficult situations.

Give me that same kind of courage, honesty, wisdom, thirst for knowledge and wisdom to understand and apply Scripture to my situations.

Give me the strength and wisdom not to be taken in by the lies and deceit of the devil, and those who live according to his values, but to always strive to do what is right.

Help me not to give your rightful place in my life to the modern idols, which are all around me in society.

Prevent me from becoming too comfortable in my faith, so that I become apathetic, complacent and compliant.

In Jesus' name. Amen.

Chapter 9 – Meeting with Giants

Unchanging God,
Thank you that you are always the same: faithful, dependable and unchanging.

Thank you that you have been faithful in the past, are faithful in the present and will continue to be faithful in the future.

Thank you that I can approach you in prayer at any time and about anything.

You know the metaphorical giants that I face *(name them)*. Help me to allow Jesus to share the burden and make my load lighter and easier to bear.

Enable me to honestly be able to pray the words 'your will be done' in all situations.

Grant me contentment and help me not to worry unnecessarily.

Inspire, guide and encourage me through words of Scripture.

Be with others, as many of them face hard times on their own. Help them to turn to you at this time.

In Jesus' name. Amen.

Chapter 10 – Growth and Maturity

Lord Jesus,
I read about your selfless and unconditional love for all people, your compassion towards those who are hurting or in need, your willingness to spend time listening to others and the way in which you share the truths of Scripture with others in wonderful simple ways – meeting people where they are.

Lord Jesus, help me to be more like you.

I thank you for Peter's courage and enthusiasm, and the way in which raw gifts such as his can be transformed and used in amazing ways, through the power of the Holy Spirit.

Lord Jesus, fill me afresh with your Holy Spirit, transform my raw gifts and use me in your kingdom.

Just as I read about the early believers being committed to you, and to things like prayer, Bible study and teaching, fellowship and sharing communion together, help me to show that same kind of commitment to the things of God, so that I might grow spiritually towards maturity – becoming more like you.

Amen.

Chapter 11 – What about the Holy Spirit?

God who loves to give good gifts to his children,

Thank you that through my repentance and faith in Jesus, you have filled me with your Holy Spirit.

Thank you that he empowers, equips, transforms and guides.

Help me to allow him freedom in every area of my life, so that he might be able to do his work within me.

Grant me the abilities necessary to fulfil my calling, and to encourage and build up others as I seek to serve you.

Anoint the natural abilities that I have, so that I might bring blessing to those whose lives you would have me touch with the love of Jesus.

In all things, help me to look to his perfect example to me during his life and ministry on earth.

Forgive me for the times when I fall short of your standards and fail to use the opportunities you put before me.

Give me courage, commitment, humility and boldness to tell others about Jesus, and through the power of your Spirit enable me to demonstrate the fruit of the Spirit in everything I say and do.

In Jesus' name. Amen.

< PAST – PRESENT – FUTURE >

Take your notebook and spend a few minutes looking back at the notes you made before the first chapter, and then jot down how you feel now:

- *What has changed in your life as a result of this journey through scripture, focusing on spirituality?*
- *Have you been able to deal with and move on from some or all of those memories from your past involving failures, difficult or sad times and regrets?*
- *In what ways has your present situation changed, for example, the job you do, family life and assessment of what you have achieved in your life so far?*
- *What about your relationship with the Triune God: God the Father, Jesus the Son and the Holy Spirit? How have these relationships changed?*
- *Finally, what about your hopes for the future, for example, your aims and priorities in life, your plans and how you would like to see yourself in five or ten years' time? Have they changed? If so, how?*